London Love Letters

Carly Lindon-Forrester

Presentation by *BookLeaf Publishing*

Web: www.bookleafpub.com

E-mail: info@bookleafpub.com

ISBN: 9789358313116

First edition 2023

To everything and everyone

PREFACE

This collection covers events from
July - October 2023.

Commune

Pixelated petals populate a triptych of TV's

A man wearing Converse stands singular in front of
the decks and begins bobbing to wicca wicca guitar,
red spot and strobes white

Deep beats
Disco streets

A man in a doo-rag dancing like he's the love child of
Pitbull and Sean Paul

3 screens shift into watered down water works akin to
Refik Anudol

Pinstripe pinafore
Too much cowbell
Smoke machine fizz
Sudden drop from hissy hi-top hiss
To space vibes and 90s pumping bass

Computer graphics transmute sea foam tower blocks
into billowing mushroom clouds of mint choc chip

A skimmed milk concentrate nightmare

Digital demolition of reconstituted high rises and
sage green spaghetti highways

Air-con high, a speck of dust flies into my eye
shattering pixels

Sudden beat change like it's the Chemical Brothers

Ginger beer
Spectral

DJ booth looks like the hull of a gnarled ship from
the 60s

Love Child sidles up to a gastric banded Guy Fieri

A barefoot skin head in a white vest and spray on
gold leggings shakes it,
shakes it all in front of the decks

Whilst hoax housing estates decay as binary echoes
of tomorrow saunter through simulated streets.

The man in spandex removes his white vest to reveal
a gold lamé bra that gloves his slithering
Iggy Pop torso.

I cannot tell if he's a performance artist or just a free
soul as he dances in front of the DJ booth and what
appears to be his ritualistic routine.

He plays lamé limbo, falls to the floor
lies on his back, limp.

Piston hip thrusts, cycle, recycle.

He then becomes enamoured with the screen to the
right of the room and dances exclusively to the digital
Rebellion

He puts his arms out wide to embrace the frame of
the LED screen as green towers return.

He is Voldo without blades and ball gag;
lithe, muscular, worn but still spectacular

A man behind the decks passes him a beer.

DJ change

A bit more disco pop then trance

Prism.

I think about making music whilst I'm forcing myself
to dance to the set; it's a bit too light hearted for me. I
like bass, garage beats and hard techno speed

I think about all the work I have to do.
I need to get back to training.

Twenty
One
Days

Who will I be in 21 days?

Dashed Hackney
Diamond Haul

I wake up hearing really big thuds, expecting to shout
at a smack head raiding the communal bins

I finger the Venetian blind and gasp
Someone is trying to break into the car outside

Astonished I grab the tassel and the cord rasps as the
bottom rail whizzes past my face

Slats clatter on this window guiro, alerting the
balaclava'd bandit

He hot wheels off into the Hoxton night cushioned by
the silence of his bike

I restore darkness to my room and return to slumber

On rising, I extract a flash card from my desk drawer
and write a note

"Someone tried to break into your vehicle at 04:30hrs
this morning"

In haste I glide out of the house in satin pyjamas and
running trainers

I cross the forecourt telling myself to wash my
pyjamas on my immediate return, not wanting the
fabric to be laced with the local air

As I approach the passenger side I see a beaded key
chain of wood dangling from the left side of the
wheel on a right hand drive Mercedes.

I frown.

I circle the bonnet and apprehend the drivers window

An encrusted seat cushion of crystal confetti
tells the scene.

Tempered auto glass once framed, is now rearranged
as a jewellery display for a hammer.

I feel it somewhat pointless to leave the note, but I
slide it under the windshield wiper anyway, with the
house number, just in case the owner would like any
further info.

They never knocked.

Stolen leather jackets

I take class in the park

Listening to life lessons about stolen leather jackets,
broom poles and broken legs

"Give me back my fucking jacket"

The sun is resplendent

We play a scene and place the protagonist,
A soon to be divorcee, in a high chair
Going through his terrible twos

"But I've gave up all opportunities to fuck other
women in my 20s to be with you, can't I,
(hyperventilates) can't I, keep the delusion that I had
a remote chance with them?"

Projectile pureed apple splatters against the tree,
My little shit, launches his Tommy Tippee
Thank god this invisible high chair is easy to clean

Afterwards, I call a friend long not seen and forever
missed. We miss each other's return calls.

I cycle home so I can prepare tomorrow's audition

The sweet smell of the pink blossom tree hits the
olfactory factoryyyyyy

I circle back to sniff that scent,
The End of Summer, eau de parfum.

A lung full, my head travels back in time to the
fuschia blossom trees of Palma.

I see my house, concrete white with its large blossom
tree outside.

Its serenity fills my heart and sings my soul.

Happiness is everywhere I go.

The day before the race

Tennis skirt and sandals 27 degrees

Gypsum pegs punctured with 56 mosquito bites

Birthday lunch with two friends before a
three hour drive

One toilet break on the road side

Police check at the border, questioned by pair

Requested to exit and open car derriere

Open boot inspection, kit all true and clean

I'm wished good luck for the race and I drive onto
the next scene

A recce for the cable car, purchase one ticket return

A 14 minute drive from Le Chable to Verbier

A 30 minute shopping trip, whizzing around Migros

A banquet for one; protein, fat and carbs

I buy some weird cheese because the illustration
makes me laugh hard

A 35 minute drive to Apartment Chez Véro et
Bernard

One owner greets me from their balcony

We two strangers make headway
With my verbal macaroni

An apartment for three, populated by me

A spotlessly clean race hub for one

Archival alpinist art splays across the wall,

One sack, one pick, two skis.

I cook myself a three course meal, finished with a
punnet of strawberries.

Zero clouds in the sky, I dine barefoot on the balcony

To start, a salad with florets of Tete de Moine,
Fromage de Bellelay

My curiosity killed the cat, it's too floral for my taste

So I extract the heads of cheese, the rest not for waste

Spinach, avo, tomato, followed by gnocchi and steak

Cow bells chime cheering as runners race through
Bourg-Saint-Pierre

I marvel at their courage and cannot wait to bear

The same determination and swigging of
Swiss fresh air

The last racer passes over crook, no one to be seen

I look down my dunes of white, blue rivers into toes

I am very much aware that I'm all on my own

I feel free and without compromise
But await the day I will analyse

Routes and races with my companion and reflect
fondly on this moment enjoying single hood.

Aiming for an early night so I'm not in
Last Minute Hell

I get to loading my race pack, waterproof and gels

I shower before 22:00 in fear of noise complaint then
clamber into bed naked, sleeping without restraint

I wake, feed, brush my teeth, kit up and load the car

I shimmy up the stairs to complete the review card

Click, lock, engage, I pull out onto the road,

I get some distance away before blasting
Beloved Techno

Today is my birthday, this gift is all for me

To put myself through my paces in 36 degrees.

London Love Letters

Home is where the heart is
And that it's obviously in my chest
I can go anywhere in the world
And know that I can rest

But London, you're something special
I really love your vibe
Magic of a South Bank sunset and
A Hackney Wick Sunrise

Bad breath Uber drivers
Smelly pits to the head on the Tube
But no matter how much I love travelling
I love it when I come back to you

Heathrow, Stansted, Gatwick,
Traipsing for the train
Black cabbing from London Bridge
Slow mo-ing Shoreditch in the rain

Raindrops on steamed windows
Traffic lights at dusk
Inspiration sweats from every corner
London you're a must

Home is where the heart is
And that it's obviously in my chest
I can go anywhere in the world

But London you're the Best!

The 9th of August

If you want perfection then go get it. But if you want

Truth

Loyalty

Passion

A Love so deep you wonder how you can come so
close to the sun and not get burned, then I'm
That Woman.

So go get perfection
See how quick that shallow pool dries.

The 13th of August

15

I wasn't looking for anything.
Then you walked into my life.

Marble Arch

My mind paints us within
several long statuary spaces

Face and breasts press against cold marble as your
warm chest pushes into my back

Wet hair cascades down my spine and you weave it
into rope as you gently pull my head back to
stipple my neck

Like Psyche revived by Cupid's kiss
I wrap your head with marmoreal wrists

A kiss.

Then a bite to my neck, alabaster turns red and your
Zaragozan almond palm beats my cheek and then
wandering fingers begin to seek,
search for ambrosia.

You marvel at my marble as my back arches with
every stroke.

I'm your living statue
No more.

Sheet music

A

Violist
Cellist
Violinist

Sit in an unclosed square and play a rather joyous
piece of music.

Animated, it paints images of a frolicking spring, an
autumnal antidote.

I study them responding to their sheet music
Curious of the composer's craft,
Timing their work so each player turns over at a
different time for continuity.

My mind denies my ignorance on musicality
And zooms in on the action, the turning of the page.

You flip me over
And follow the clef on my clavicle
Inking kisses across my neck, completing a stanza,
before playing my left scapula, enjoying the sensation
of your lips
on my skin

The violinist shake her heads exuberantly

You whip the duvet into a fresh cover
I admire you making the space ready for play.
Welcoming, caring, fresh.

As I daydream, I look up and out of the ample
windows and the music turns murderous.
I see a white light in the top stairwell of a
Clerkenwell apartment block.

My eyes scan to the right and the only occupied
apartment is lit in red.

Rosemary's Baby.

A figure slings itself out the window and
into the street.

A red double decker passes.

The trio conclude their concert.

All the narratives come to an end.

An artist sat behind me asks me what I thought about
the performance…I tell him everything the music
helped me to see, apart from what was once real.

A rare creature

Green Eyes 2%
Personality type 2%

Sigh.

Enraptured

My body is a kite
I'm flying high above the
Sinister plinky plonk nightmare

Love it

Pizzicato taking the piss
Strings plucking events from my mind,
It's another scene,
from another film,
from another life.

I return to my denim'd body sat on the
hard wooden chair.

Curious about others enjoyment,
I glance at an audience member,
Her mouth agape in awe at the violin and voice.
She wouldn't look out of place in a bingo hall.

I wonder if there's been an opera in a bingo hall.
Which reminds me of a scene from Better Call Saul
Jimmy McGill tickling bingo balls.

I remember being a bingo caller once. Depressing.
Although quite humorous if the crowd's right.

The recital ends. The composer talks and says

"When you're listening for mistakes, you're missing
the music"

A truth bomb explodes like an an egg in a microwave
on to my face. I laugh, no-one else can see it but me.

Humpty Numpty.

I realise now how much I missed our music.
But then,

I am observant.
I see it all.
And I'm single
Because I see it all.

Draw a line under it

Quick witted bimbo

I'm like a hot comedian, I make you giggle and sweaty all at the same time, then I take the bin-bag off to give you a breather.

(This line gets a lot of hits on Hinge)

Pale patient pigeon

Pale patient pigeon pink in plume
Basques in the shadow of a Monday afternoon
Cast along sand coloured aggregate
That blends with the banks of the South.

She's still
She stares
Her breast is full
Feathers ruffled from the rough and tumble

Her beady little orange fixates on me
Together we play psychic eye spy.

Left foot missing a digit
But Patient Pink,
she doesn't fidget

I rise from the bench
She doesn't flinch
I stretch out my arms
then step forward an inch

Still
She lets me photograph her
As she elongates into that feminine shape
Wings without bars and
That Iridescent nape

Forever the model
she peeks over her scapula,
knowing that poses
look better when angular.

Pale patient pigeon pink in plume
Hobbles under the bench all too soon
That's a wrap! The day is done so
I return to sky gazing
And the man made pigeons.

Black Beauty

Her name is Black Beauty.

She's a nippy little single speed.

Battered like a whore from Hoxton; she's not the
same gal as when I first laid eyes on her.

Some fucker ripped her headset off
three days into purchase

A few years later someone whipped the carbon fibre
gel seat, which was perfect for me

Because this owner is no fat bottom girl, wide seats
are a no-go Freddie.

So now BB, she's a black patchwork, battered and
bruised so people leave her alone.

My treasure.

The Man in the bathroom

He watches over me
Every time I brush my teeth

A tall man of discoloured emulsion
Cream stains coming through white

His head a hardened lump of paint, hairless

An ominous figure but he's so small that if I hadn't of
noticed him, he wouldn't exist at all.

Tall
Long over coat with wide collar
Tea stained shoulders
Of aged paint
Shirt and tie
Never ending legs
And the bag he carries is circular
Perhaps he's carrying vinyl or a cymbal

Sometimes I wonder
How he came to be trapped in paint
In this bathroom
What did he do so wrong to be here?
He sees all manner of brushing, washing, scrubbing
and pissing.

Bare breasts in the mirror as I cleanse my face

Limp penises emerging from trousers as skinny
bodies and plump arses climb into the shower beyond
his peripheral vision.

He's seen useless repair men come back several times
to fix the same fucking job

His vista is of a chrome radiator and an air vent that
can't circulate shit but blows blue Hoxton dust in his
face on the daily

Our activities brighten his day (the little perv) but
then he's bored because they're typically the same.

The ritual of hygiene.

18th October 2023

You send me a video at 07:48
3 days and 20 minutes after we three, peeled
ourselves away from Charterhouse Street.

52 seconds of haze, lights and silhouettes
You've captured a moment of me in active peace
As one of two pony-tailed brunettes swishing our
manes to the beats

A stranger to the left, my long lost dancing twin
His boyfriend in white chino's watching over him
As he and I in duplicate rave
To Love Panda - Metro Circuit on the Room 1 stage

I am so pleased you captured this moment
Because that track hit me like a recurring omen.

When I dance I feel my soul.

46.0961° N, 7.2286° E

Battered in Bagnes
Bouncing off boulders
Bombing down quarries
Bounding through forests with tap dance dexterity
Braving thirty-six degree heat
Best day of my life.

Slipping and spraining on a Swiss afternoon
Could not detract from the fact that
I have never felt so free.

My medallion,
A tiger's eye veneered toe
Still present in a slow October.

No where to hide

Swan necks of orient bent
Meander through fresco torment
Wings thrash heaving leafy carriages
Dragging stumped seraphs to safety

Torsos swaddled in calico
Angelic injuries replete
Carbon copy carnage
A pyrrhic victory

Digitised dust and decoration
A centrefold of hell
But a fracture cements my attention
And breaks the mirrored spell

Perfection cracked
Interest remains
Pitch black
A bear on the reins

Chiaroscuro cherubim
Emerge from oxidised blood
A lion unleashed
Guided by palm

A demon displayed
Screams from a vase
A small boy dreams
From it's forehead

Who are these players
When the boy awakes?
How does he survive this dread?
Am I too in his magnificent dream?

Or should I go back to bed?

White, green & navy

"Who goes there? Is it the Knight of Night?"

"Well yes, my fair maiden it is he"

"What time do you return tomorrow morning?"

"11am"

"Then come here, make love to me"

"But you're head deep dreaming my love"

"And now it's a waking dream"

Fingers fondle forest green silk
Strapping palms brush over alabaster
Gliding up over marble ridges
To slip under camisole & caress white hot orbs

A star cracks open my sternum
Molten gold rises from the solar plexus
Gilding my throat as pitch black pupils turn auric
Two suns radiate, encircled in galaxies green

A breath to the ear guides my head left,
Lips burning, hips turning towards light years of love
I freeze facing the furnace, a sight to behold
Two suns emanating gold, bound by galaxies blue

Burnished lips bridge a path from
Adam's apple to pineal point

1046 degrees celsius and rising

Fingertips grip your muscular frame
Pulling you through me and you snap back
As I pluck the band on your navy shorts
Releasing a gods roar, rumbling

But I do not quake
You gather me up into your palms
And you wear me as your crown

A pallet knife and
pixelated pigment

2B193D - Blackcurrant:
To be nineteen in third position.

2C365E - Bay of Many:
To see three, sixty-five year old evangelists convene
in a curve

484D6D - East Bay:
484 towards Camberwell green, a used Caterpillar
D6D, Japan undercarriage: 92% clean

4B8F8C - Blue Chi:
Forbearance ate through ecstasy, for bait to seal fate
sacrifices agency

C5979D - Careys pink:
See thighs dressed to the nines seven steps to heaven
nine circles to hell. Dead.